Hurricanes

By Jim Mezzanotte

Science and curriculum consultant: Debra Voege, M.A., science and math curriculum resource teacher

Reading specialist: Linda Cornwell, Literacy Connections Consulting

WEEKLY READER®
PUBLISHING

Please visit our web site at **www.garethstevens.com**.
For a free color catalog describing our list of high-quality books,
call 1-800-542-2595 (USA) or 1-800-387-3178 (Canada).
Our fax: (877) 542-2596

Library of Congress Cataloging-in-Publication Data

Mezzanotte, Jim.
    Hurricanes / by Jim Mezzanotte ; science and curriculum consultant, Debra Voege.
       p. cm. — (Wild weather)
    Includes bibliographical references and index.
    ISBN-10: 1-4339-2348-3   ISBN-13: 978-1-4339-2348-7 (lib. bdg.)
    ISBN-10: 1-4339-2362-9   ISBN-13: 978-1-4339-2362-3 (pbk.)
    1. Hurricanes—Juvenile literature. I. Title.
    QC944.2.M493   2010
    551.55'2—dc22   2009001975

This edition first published in 2010 by
Weekly Reader® Books
An Imprint of Gareth Stevens Publishing
1 Reader's Digest Road
Pleasantville, NY 10570-7000 USA

Copyright © 2010 by Gareth Stevens, Inc.

Executive Managing Editor: Lisa M. Herrington
Senior Editor: Barbara Bakowski
Creative Director: Lisa Donovan
Designer: Melissa Welch, *Studio Montage*
Photo Researcher: Diane Laska-Swanke

Photo credits: Cover, title © Lynne Barrows/Shutterstock; pp. 3, 4, 8, 14, 18, 22, 24
© Zaporozhchenko Yury/Shutterstock; p. 5 © Nada Pecnik/Visuals Unlimited; pp. 10, 11, 12 NOAA;
pp. 6, 17, 19 © AP Images; p. 7 Tammy West/© Gareth Stevens, Inc.; p. 9, Scott M. Krall/© Gareth
Stevens, Inc.; p. 13 © Tyler Olson/Shutterstock; p. 15 © Mark Harmel/Photo Researchers, Inc.; p. 16
© Rob & Ann Simpson/Visuals Unlimited; p. 21 © Tad Denson/Shutterstock

Printed in the United States of America

1 2 3 4 5 6 7 8 9 10 12 11 10 09

Table of Contents

Words in **boldface** are defined in the glossary.

CHAPTER 1
Here Comes a Hurricane!

Strong winds begin to blow. Giant waves crash onto the land. Heavy rains fall. A **hurricane** is coming!

Hurricane clouds form near the coast.

Hurricanes are the largest and most powerful storms. They form over oceans in warm places.

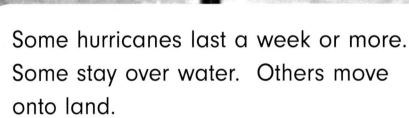

Some hurricanes last a week or more. Some stay over water. Others move onto land.

Hurricanes hit the United States between June and November. Hurricanes form in other parts of the world, too.

This map shows the path taken by Hurricane Katrina in 2005.

CHAPTER 2
Hurricanes in Action

The Sun heats the water in warm oceans and seas. Some of the water turns into a **gas** called **water vapor.**

Warm air and water vapor rise. High
in the sky, the vapor cools. It turns
into drops of water. The drops form
rain clouds.

drops
of water

water
vapor

ocean

Warm air and water vapor rise. Clouds form when
vapor cools and turns into water drops.

Strong winds begin blowing. They spin in a circle. Heavy rains fall. A hurricane is born!

eye

This is Hurricane Katrina, as seen from space.

The center of a hurricane is called the **eye.** It has few clouds and little wind. Sometimes, people are fooled by the eye. They think the hurricane is over.

Special pilots fly planes into the eye of a hurricane. They get information about the size and strength of the storm.

Soon the wind and rain are back.
Rings of rain clouds circle the eye.
The winds are strongest in the ring
closest to the eye.

When a hurricane reaches land, it starts
to get weaker. Soon, the storm ends.

CHAPTER 3
Deadly Hurricanes

Hurricanes can destroy towns and kill people. In 1900, a hurricane hit Texas. It killed more people than any other hurricane in the United States.

Strong winds tear off roofs and break windows. The winds can pick up cars, boats, and even houses!

Hurricane Katrina ruined many homes. This house was blown on top of a car.

Heavy rain and high waves cause **floods.** Rivers and lakes overflow. Hills may come sliding down.

High waves can sweep away homes on the coast.

Rescue workers help people
who are hurt or trapped.
Soon, people can clean up.
They rebuild homes, bridges,
and roads.

Floods can trap people
in their homes. Rescue
workers take them to a
safe place.

CHAPTER 4

Hurricane Safety

Scientists use special tools to watch for storms. When winds reach a certain speed, the storms become hurricanes! If a hurricane is headed for land, the scientists warn people.

How do people stay safe from hurricanes?
If a storm is coming, they board up
windows. They take everything inside.

Hurricane Supply List

- First aid kit and medicines

- Canned food and can opener

- Bottled water

- Food for pets

- Radio, flashlight, and extra batteries

- Raincoats and boots

- Blankets, pillows, and sleeping bags

People may have to leave their homes for safer places. Some people go to a **shelter.** A shelter is a strong building where they can stay during a storm.

Today, fewer people die in hurricanes than in the past. We know when a hurricane is coming. We can get ready and stay safe!

Glossary

eye: the calm center of a hurricane

floods: overflows of water onto land that is usually dry

gas: a form (such as water vapor) that is not solid (like ice) or liquid (like water). A gas has no shape. It usually cannot be seen.

hurricane: a storm with very high winds and heavy rain

shelter: a safe place where people can stay in an emergency

water vapor: water in the form of a gas

For More Information

Books

Hurricane Hunters! Riders on the Storm. Chris L. Demarest (Margaret K. McElderry, 2006)

Story of a Storm: A Book About Hurricane Katrina. Reona Visser (Quail Ridge Press, 2006)

Yesterday We Had a Hurricane. Deirdre McLaughlin Mercier (Bumble Bee Publishing, 2006)

Web Sites

FEMA for Kids: Hurricanes
www.fema.gov/kids/hurr
Find facts, quizzes, and videos.

Miami Museum of Science: Hurricane
www.miamisci.org/hurricane
Learn about planes that fly into hurricanes.

Publisher's note to educators and parents: Our editors have carefully reviewed these web sites to ensure that they are suitable for children. Many web sites change frequently, however, and we cannot guarantee that a site's future contents will continue to meet our high standards of quality and educational value. Be advised that children should be closely supervised whenever they access the Internet.

Index

About the Author

Jim Mezzanotte has written many books for children. He lives in Milwaukee, Wisconsin, with his wife and two sons. He has always been interested in weather, especially big storms.

Caterpillars

by **Trudi Strain Trueit**

Reading Consultant: Nanci R. Vargus, Ed.D.

Marshall Cavendish
Benchmark
New York

Picture Words

 branch

 butterfly

 caterpillar

 caterpillars

flower

 grass

 hand

 leaf

 rock

 are busy!

A  can creep

in the ____.

A 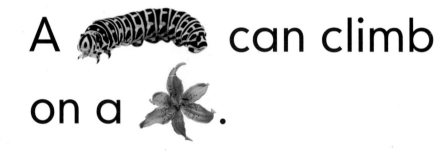 can climb on a .

A  can rest

on a .

A  can sit

on your .

A  can munch

on a .

A  can crawl
on a ⎯ᒣ.

A 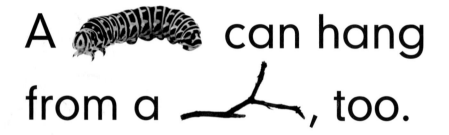 can hang from a ⌐L, too.

A  can become a !